The Witch's Things
A Counting to 20 Rhyme

by Spencer Brinker

Consultant:
Kimberly Brenneman, PhD
National Institute for Early Education Research
Rutgers University
New Brunswick, New Jersey

BEARPORT
PUBLISHING

New York, New York

Credits

Publisher: Kenn Goin
Editorial Director: Adam Siegel
Senior Editor: Joyce Tavolacci
Creative Director: Spencer Brinker
Photo Illustrations: Kim Jones and Bearport Publishing

Library of Congress Cataloging-in-Publication Data

Brinker, Spencer, author.
  The witch's things : a counting to 20 rhyme / by Spencer Brinker.
      pages cm.—(Spooky math)
  Includes bibliographical references and index.
  ISBN 978-1-62724-333-9 (library binding)—ISBN 1-62724-333-X (library binding)
  1. Counting—Juvenile literature. 2. Witches—Juvenile literature. I. Title.
  QA113.B6875 2015
  513.2'1—dc23

2014004647

For more information, write to Bearport Publishing Company, Inc., 45 West 21st Street, Suite 3B, New York, New York 10010. Printed in the United States of America.

10 9 8 7 6 5 4 3 2 1

Contents

A Counting Witch

My name is Belinda—
I'm a witch, don't you see?

I truly love counting.
Come try it with me.

witch bane

I live in **one** castle
with **two** creepy towers.

Can you find the **three** ghosts?
They howl at all hours.

My door has **four** knockers.
They're shiny and bright.

Instead of a welcome,
they cause quite a fright.

This room has **five** cauldrons with potions inside.

Can you find the **six** toads? Some are long. Some are wide.

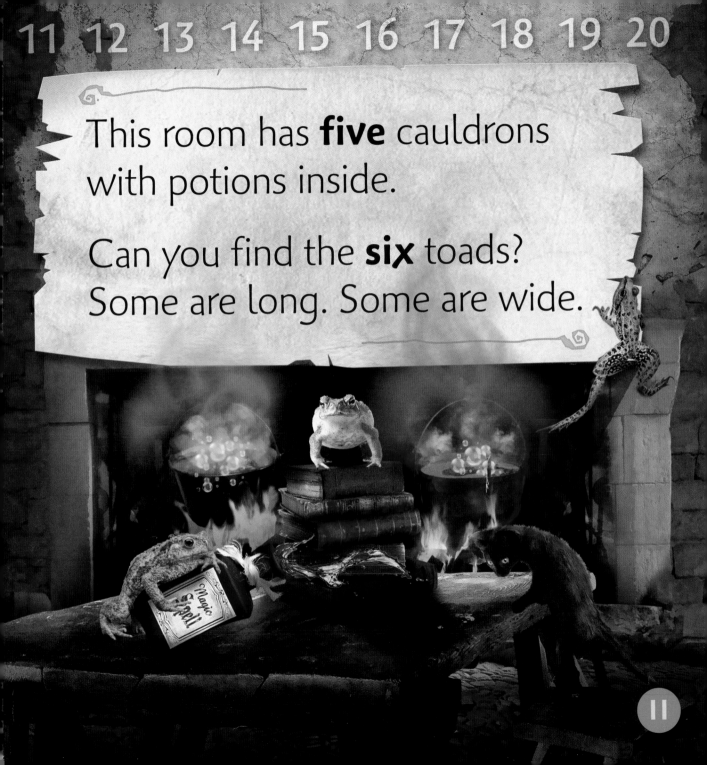

Among dirty dishes
hide several small friends.

Can you spot **seven** mice
with **eight** tails at their ends?

My toes sometimes tickle.
I look for some clues.

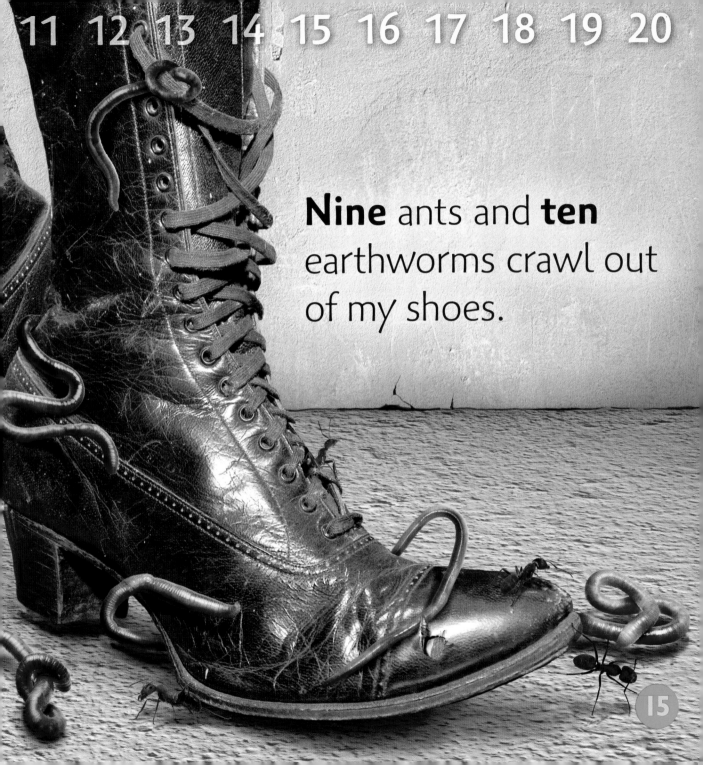

Nine ants and **ten** earthworms crawl out of my shoes.

Eleven tall candles are found in this hall.

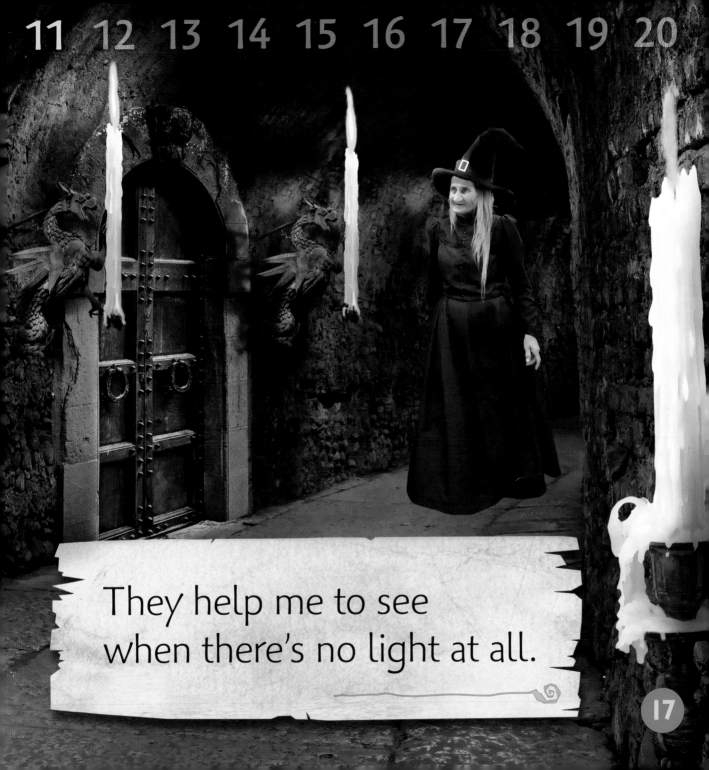

They help me to see
when there's no light at all.

My drawer holds **twelve** socks, but just one matching pair.

18

The pink ones with stripes are my favorite to wear.

I have **thirteen** cats.
Their eyes glow a
bright green.

When they meow all together,
they cause quite a scene!

21

1 2 3 4 5 6 7 8 9 10

This shelf has my spell books, **fourteen** in a row.

22

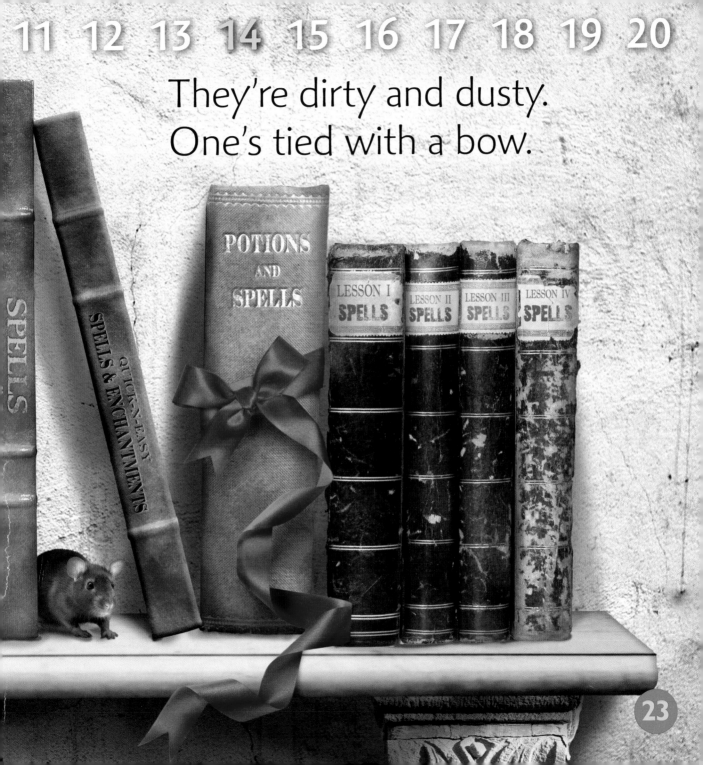

They're dirty and dusty.
One's tied with a bow.

I head out the door
on my way to a scare.

Fifteen hats I can choose from.
Sixteen scarves I can wear.

My brooms aren't for cleaning.
Instead they can fly!

I have **seventeen** brooms
that can soar through the sky.

Near **eighteen** short toadstools sit **nineteen** pumpkins with eyes!

Can you count **twenty** spiders, each catching some flies?

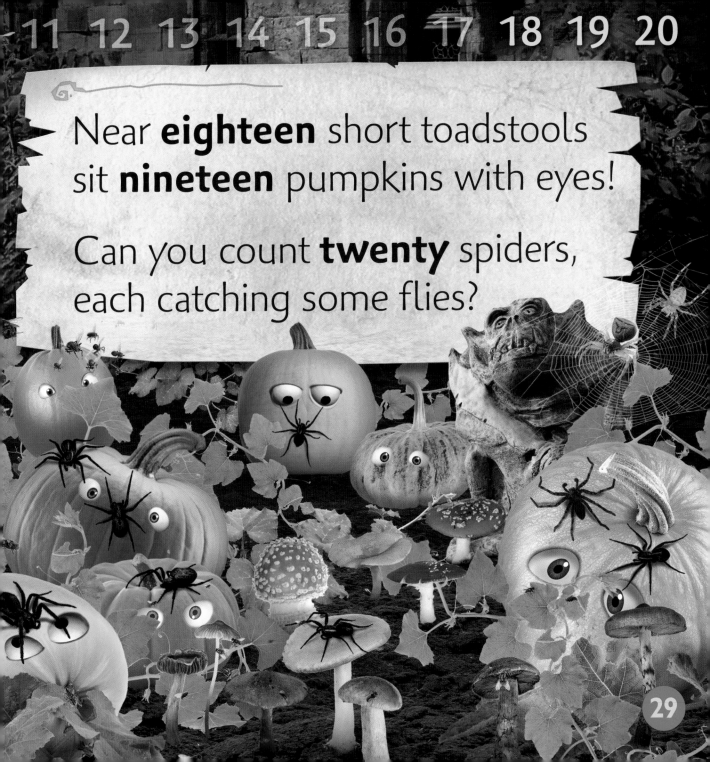

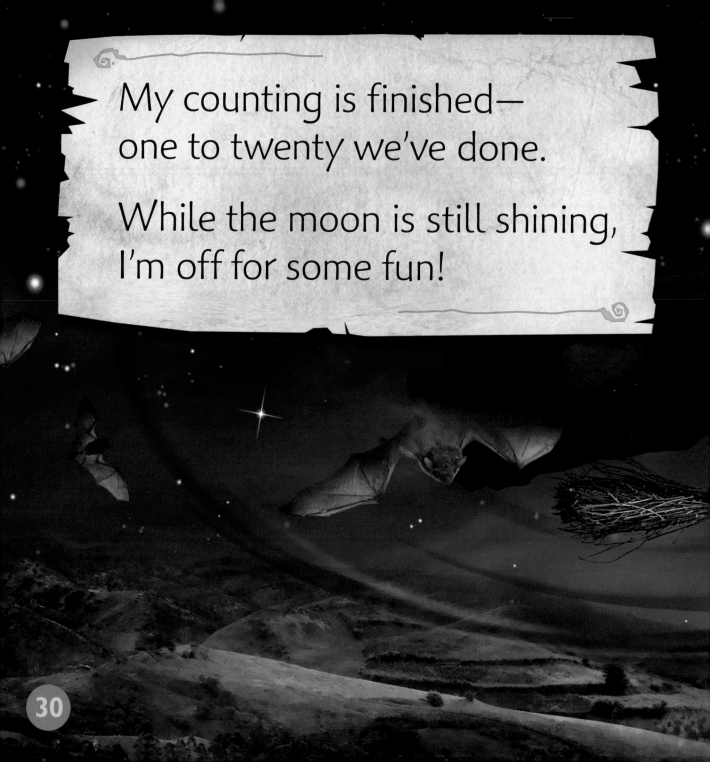

My counting is finished—
one to twenty we've done.

While the moon is still shining,
I'm off for some fun!

Read More

Capote, Lori. *Monster Knows Numbers* (*Monster Knows Math*). North Mankato, MN: Capstone (2013).

Yoon, Salina. *One Halloween Night: A Spooky Seek-and-Count Book*. New York: Sterling (2011).

Learn More Online

To learn more about counting and numbers, visit
www.bearportpublishing.com/SpookyMath

About the Author

Spencer Brinker lives and works in New York City, where he counts subway stops, traffic lights, and taxi cabs. Unfortunately, the only broom he has is used for cleaning.